There are only two ways to live your life.
One is as though nothing is a miracle.
The other is as though everything is a miracle.

ALBERT EINSTEIN

The Gift of Miracles
Copyright © 2007 by Zondervan
ISBN: 978-0-310-81183-1

Requests for information should be addressed to:
Inspirio, the gift group of Zondervan
Grand Rapids, Michigan 49530
www.inspiriogifts.com

Compiler: SnapdragonGroup℠ Editorial Services
Project Manager: Kim Zeilstra
Design Manager: Michael J. Williams
Production Management: Matt Nolan
Design: Brand Navigation, www.brandnavigation.com

Printed in China
07 08 09 / 4 3 2 1

The GIFT of MIRACLES

INSPIRING MODERN DAY *and* BIBLICAL WONDERS

inspirio®

*A miracle is an event beyond the power
of any known physical law to produce;
it is a spiritual occurrence produced
by the power of God,
a marvel, a wonder.*

BILLY GRAHAM

Contents

INTRODUCTION

Miracles are an integral part of the Bible text. There are more than 150 accounts of miracles sprinkled throughout the Old and New Testaments. Taken together, they cover the spectrum of human need—healing, protection, provision, intervention, deliverance, and personal transformation. The blind regained their sight, the lame felt their legs strengthened and walked, the Red Sea parted so that runaway slaves could escape from their enemies, ravens delivered food to a down-and-out prophet, snakebites were rendered harmless, the raging sea was tamed, and many who were dead drew their breath again. That's just for starters.

Within these pages, we have worked to illuminate the nature and characteristics of biblical miracles, both through biblical accounts and through stories of miracles experienced by everyday people just like you. We hope that as you read, you will see that miracles are a recurring element of the Christian experience today, tomorrow, and for the remainder of our days here on Earth.

BIBLICAL TRUTHS
ABOUT MIRACLES

—Genuine miracles are beneficial, instructive, and worthy of God as their author.

—Genuine miracles attest to and are supported by sound biblical doctrine.

—Genuine miracles inspire worship of God and are reflective of his character.

—Genuine miracles are consistent with the broad scheme of revelation throughout the Old and New Testament.

Miracles are the great bell of the universe, which draws men to God's sermon.

JOHN FOSTER

―――――― ❦ ――――――

"I will restore you to health
and heal your wounds,"
declares the LORD.

JEREMIAH 30:17

―――――― ❦ ――――――

MIRACLES OF
DIVINE HEALING

—⁂—

*"Lord,... stretch out your hand
to heal and perform signs and
wonders through the name of
your holy servant Jesus."*

ACTS 4:29–30 TNIV

—⁂—

Heal me, O LORD, and I will be healed;
  save me and I will be saved,
for you are the one I praise.

JEREMIAH 17:14

Sometimes the Lord disturbs
  the waters before sending
    his healing angel.

JOHN HARPER

MIRACLES OF DIVINE HEALING

"WHAT'S FOR DINNER?"

"Hello, Mother, what's for dinner? I'm starved!"

Those were Dad's first words every night when he walked in the door, and every night Mom would sigh, wipe her hands on her apron, and say, "Oh, Robert, really! Can't you even say hello first?" And he'd say with a grin, "I did, honey. Now what's for dinner?" He'd give her a quick kiss on the cheek and she'd go back to making dinner. The routine was comforting.

It was 1948, and we lived in a small Minnesota town about ninety miles west of Minneapolis. Dad worked a hard ten-hour day at the major industry, the Land O' Lakes plant. His salary could barely support a wife and five children, but he never complained. He just thanked God that he had a job. And he thanked him that his family was healthy and that church was within walking distance and that the potatoes had a good crop this year and … well, you get the picture. He was a thankful man.

MIRACLES OF DIVINE HEALING

I think we were probably poor, but we didn't know it. We didn't have a car or one fancy thing in our home, but neither did most of the people we knew. Our social life consisted of extended family gatherings and church, lots of church—Sunday morning, Sunday evening, and Wednesday evening. Once when I asked Dad why we had to go to church so often, he said, "Honey, we don't *have* to; we *get* to. There are lots of people in the world who don't have that privilege." I didn't think it was such a privilege but if Dad said so, then I guess I believed it, too.

That was pretty much our life—simple, happy, probably boring by most standards. But there would come a day when we would long for boring.

It was a September day, and Mom was ironing—seemed like she was always ironing. But with a husband, a 7-year old, a 5-year old, a 3-year old, and 16-month-old twins—long before the days of permanent-press clothes—it was an unending chore. The phone rang and her face went white. Dad had collapsed at work after complaining of a headache,

MIRACLES OF
DIVINE HEALING

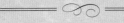

and those around him had quickly called for an ambulance.

Mom called the pastor and then my uncle. Within minutes, a lady from church arrived to stay with us and Uncle Andy came to drive Mom to the hospital. Mom and Dad waited together for the doctor to deliver the diagnosis, and when it came, it wasn't good. The doctor held up the x-ray, and Mom told us later that the large and odd-shaped tumor was clearly visible even to her untrained eye. The doctor wasn't sure that the tumor was operable, but he had made arrangements to have Dad transferred to a major hospital in Minneapolis for further diagnosis and treatment. Then the man of medicine looked at them both and said grimly, "If you believe in miracles, this would be a good time to start praying for one."

Mom went in the ambulance with Dad, one hand holding his, the other clutching the X-rays. Our pastor followed in his car. Physician after physician came in and gave the same diagnosis. The tumor was growing rapidly and pushing against the cortex

MIRACLES OF DIVINE HEALING

of his brain, the section that controls motor skills. Surgery was needed, the sooner the better. The physicians didn't mince words; the surgery was very risky, and even if they could get it all, the prognosis wasn't good. They felt Dad's brain had already been badly damaged—life expectancy would be short and that of little quality. He might even be left in a "vegetative state."

The operation was scheduled for the next morning. Because my baby brother had pneumonia and the twins had the flu, Dad convinced Mom—in spite of her protests—to go home and be with us. "It's all in God's hands anyway," he assured her. The pastor would stay with him and keep us informed. Mom told us later that the three of them prayed for a long time and talked about things important and mundane. Finally, amid tears and against her better judgment, Mom took the bus back home.

The next morning we began by praying for Dad and tried to go about our normal activities. But nothing was normal without our dad. Neighbors

MIRACLES OF
DIVINE HEALING

came by to sit with us and pray. The church secretary organized a nonstop prayer chain. Mom watched the clock and checked several times to see if it was really working—11:00, 12:00, 1:00, 2:00. We knew what she was thinking, *The surgery should be over by now. Why hasn't the pastor called?*

Not knowing what else to do, Mom did what she always did—set up the ironing board and went to work. After a few minutes, I saw her gaze out the big picture window and gasp. For a moment I thought the iron would drop to the floor. As if in slow motion, she turned, set the iron back onto the board, and then moved toward the door with all of us right behind her.

It seemed like time stopped. We couldn't believe our eyes. Dad was walking up the sidewalk toward us, arms open wide!

When the shock and excitement had subsided somewhat, Dad told us all the story. Early that morning, the surgeons had ordered another set of X-rays—a routine, pre-op formality. They suspected

MIRACLES OF
DIVINE HEALING

an error when the new X-ray revealed no trace of a tumor. Another set of X-rays were taken … and another … but there was still no tumor.

Instead of going to the operating room, Dad had been discharged—the doctors reluctantly acknowledging that some sort of miracle had taken place. Dad and our pastor had taken the bus home from Minneapolis. And true to form, Dad's first words had been "Hello, Mother, what's for dinner? I'm starved!"

Dad lived another forty-eight years with no recurrence or symptoms.[1]

MIRACLES OF
DIVINE HEALING

*The head of medical service in a great
university hospital once said, "One
should send for his minister
(or priest or rabbi) as he sends for his
doctor when he becomes ill." That
is to say, God helps the sick in two
ways—through the science of
medicine and surgery and through the
science of faith and prayer.*

NORMAN VINCENT
PEALE

MIRACLES OF DIVINE HEALING

*No one ever looks in vain to the
Great Physician.*

F. F. BOSWORTH

MIRACLES OF DIVINE HEALING

A MIRACLE FOR MELODIE

My heart was pounding like it was going to burst right out of my chest. I anxiously paced in and out of the electronic door, holding my hands tightly to my chest.

"Why, God? Why did this have to happen?" I muttered under my breath. An ambulance siren pierced the quiet darkness.

Before the paramedics could get the ambulance doors opened, I was on top of them, pushing and demanding to know, "Where is my baby? Is she all right?"

Someone pulled me out of the way as the paramedics moved my daughter from the stretcher to a gurney and communicated her condition to the hospital's medical personnel. Within a matter of seconds, she was whisked away, and all I was able to see was her little blonde ringlets and half her body packed in ice.

"We need a miracle," I heard my husband say at one point to no one in particular. He was right. Our

MIRACLES OF DIVINE HEALING

precious two-year-old daughter had been severely scalded. The doctors told us later that Melodie had suffered third-degree burns over one entire side of her face and second-degree burns down her neck and the entirety of her left arm. We needed a miracle in the worst way.

Earlier that evening, I never would have guessed that things could go so wrong. It was a few days before Christmas and bitter cold outside. We were about ready to leave for church, and I had put a pan of water on the stove for tea. It seemed like a good idea to take a hot cup along with me on the cold ride. I quickly placed the diaper bag and the stroller in the car. That's when I heard the screams.

My heart sank into my stomach as I sprinted into the house and down the hall to the kitchen. There I found our Melodie sprawled on the floor, kicking her little legs and flailing her arms. I shouted for my husband as I fumbled to remove Melodie's coat and velvet bonnet. When Rick appeared, he took one look and knew we needed help — fast.

MIRACLES OF
DIVINE HEALING

"Forget everything else," he yelled, "Get in the car now! Move it!"

I climbed into the front seat, and Rick placed Melodie in my arms.

At the neighborhood Emergency Medical Center, Rick took our baby and rushed inside. I parked the car and hurried to get inside the center, where I ran face-first into my husband who was rushing back out the entrance.

"What's happening?" I asked in a panic. "Where's Melodie?"

"It's bad, honey! A lot worse than we thought," he answered, taking me firmly by the arm and rushing me toward the parking lot. "They are packing her face in ice and taking her by ambulance to the county hospital."

"You take the car," he shouted, "and I'll ride in the ambulance and meet you at the hospital."

The drive to the hospital seemed endless. *What was I thinking?* I asked myself. *How could I have done*

MIRACLES OF
DIVINE HEALING

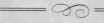

such a stupid thing? "Please, dear God! Please let my baby be all right. Please don't let her die," I pleaded.

The hours were long and agonizing before we were allowed to see her. She had been sedated, and I was relieved that she seemed to be sleeping. Any comfort ended there. An IV needle protruded from her little arm, and the skin was completely gone from her face, exposing swollen weeping tissue where the water had splashed and burned her. Her lips were almost a third of the size of her entire face; her tongue swollen many times its normal size.

The doctor explained that they had begun a regimen of antibiotics to lower the risk of infection. As soon as she was stabilized, we were told, she would undergo her first surgery. Ten days passed before that happened—ten agonizing days for Melodie, for Rick, and for me.

During that time, we had two notable visitors, each suggesting very different outcomes for Melodie in the days ahead. One visitor—a hospital psychia-

MIRACLES OF
DIVINE HEALING

trist—showed us pictures of burn victims. He gave us the painful, heart-wrenching news that Melodie would have to have multiple surgeries and skin grafts on her face every year until she was well into her twenties. Just hearing her prognosis was an excruciating, unbearable reality.

The second visitor was a friend who encouraged us to call the pastor to come and pray for her to be healed. When we expressed doubt that prayer could possibly change our situation, she responded, "What do you have to lose?"

The pastor came to see us—at our request—the night before Melodie's first surgery. Walking in with a Bible under his arm, he consoled us for a few minutes and then asked if he could read us a verse. Opening his Bible to the book of James, he began to read from chapter five, "Is any one of you sick? He should call the elders of the church to pray over him and anoint him with oil in the name of the Lord. And the prayer offered in faith will make the sick person well; the Lord will raise him up."

MIRACLES OF DIVINE HEALING

"This is God's promise to you," the pastor continued. "Melodie is precious to him." With our permission, Pastor anointed Melodie with oil and prayed for her to be healed, while Rick and I looked on.

The next day, Melodie was wheeled away to the operating room for her first of twenty or more surgeries. Hours later when they brought her back to her room, her whole head was wrapped in gauze bandages like a little mummy. All we could see were two holes for her eyes and her painfully burnt swollen lips. The nurse told me that it would be twenty-four hours before the bandages would be changed.

All night, I dreaded seeing her face for the first time. The psychologist had warned that some parents couldn't handle it. Now we were here, watching as the nurse snipped away at the bandages, little by little, with fresh gauze and ointment ready to be applied. "I can already see that her lips are much better," she said as she worked.

Then I heard her gasp, as she moved so that we could better see the little face as she unwound

MIRACLES OF
DIVINE HEALING

the bandages. Without speaking, we watched in utter amazement. Melodie's face was completely healed—as pink as a rose and as smooth and soft as silk. In fact, it was so completely healed that it actually looked like the doctors had wrapped up a well baby in gauze for no reason.

Grabbing Melodie in my arms, Rick and I danced around the room, overcome by joy and wonder. "Hallelujah, sweet Melodie," I heard Rick say. "There really are miracles!"[2]

MIRACLES OF DIVINE HEALING

"*Worship the* LORD *your God, and
his blessing will be on your food and
water. I will take away sickness from
among you.*"

EXODUS 23:25

MIRACLES OF DIVINE HEALING

HEALING PRAYER

"Mom," Julie Anne's voice was nearly as still as the night. But I awakened as readily as if she had shouted. It had been that way between us ever since Julie's birth twenty-eight years earlier.

"What is it, honey?" I raised myself onto one elbow from the cot where I lay in the semi-dark hospital room. Sleeping fitfully throughout the night, my daughter's labored breathing and intermittent groans had become a part of my worrisome nightmares.

"I'm dying, Mom," Julie said softly. "I can sense it," she whispered, "and I just want you to know that I'm ok with it … with dying, I mean."

I sprang to my feet and leaned over the hospital bed looking into my child's face, studying the pale, sallow appearance that seemed just as it had been earlier in the evening. For the past three days it had grown progressively worse.

MIRACLES OF DIVINE HEALING

"I'm calling the nurse," I announced, reaching for the call button.

Julie Anne and her husband, Brian, had arrived five days ago, on the Saturday prior to Christmas. Home for the holidays and three months pregnant, a spirit of celebration and joy had permeated the family gathering.

But on Sunday, Julie fell ill with a kidney infection. By late afternoon, her fever had spiked so high that we had rushed her to the emergency room. We had expected to take Julie home with medication, but the doctors insisted on admitting her.

The fever persisted. While undergoing treatment for the kidney infection, Julie was over-hydrated—complicating the situation with the development of pneumonia by the third day.

Responding to her concern, the floor nurse put in an urgent call to a local specialist. I was uneasy with the eeriness of the atmosphere as medical personnel scurried about in the wee hours of the morning.

Miracles of Divine Healing

Frowning as a result of his examination, Julie's new doctor ordered a chest X-ray, explaining that he suspected a blood clot.

Phoning home, I awakened my husband, Stan.

"Honey," I spoke softly, hoping Julie wouldn't overhear me, "we have a dire situation here. The doctor is concerned that Julie Anne might have a blood clot. Her life and the baby's life could be in danger. I need you to call Phil and Mac immediately. We need our godly men to come pray over her."

Stan and I had never known men of greater faith than Phil Robertson and Mac Owen, two of the spiritual leaders in our church. Just minutes after the orderlies had wheeled Julie Anne back into her room, they joined us at her bedside.

"Father," Phil began in his familiar way. "You see us standing here over this young woman. Now Father, she is carrying a child and I suppose her body doesn't have the strength to fight the way it should. Lord, there isn't any point in mincing words, we just need you to do what you do best—heal her, Father."

MIRACLES OF
DIVINE HEALING

Phil finished with a resounding finale, "Lord, we have the courage to make this request boldly in the name of the one who overcame death on our behalf—Jesus. Amen."

No sooner had they all lifted their heads, but Julie Anne opened her eyes and smiled. Looking around the bed, she grew concerned, "What's going on? Why are you all kneeling?"

As she spoke, I noticed color returning to Julie's cheeks. I felt her forehead with the back of my hand and knew instantly that her fever was gone.

Julie Anne was released the next morning. The pneumonia was gone, the fever never returned. As I wheeled my daughter down the hall and out the door, I whispered a prayer of gratitude for the miraculous rescue of not one, but two precious lives.[3]

MIRACLES OF DIVINE HEALING

Is any one of you in trouble? He should pray. Is anyone happy? Let him sing songs of praise. Is any one of you sick? He should call the elders of the church to pray over him and anoint him with oil in the name of the Lord. And the prayer offered in faith will make the sick person well; the Lord will raise him up.

JAMES 5:13–15

MIRACLES OF DIVINE HEALING

A miracle in the sense of the New Testament is not so much a breach of the laws of nature, but rather a remarkable or exceptional occurrence which brought an undeniable sense of the presence and power of God.

C. H. DODD

MIRACLES OF DIVINE HEALING

THE VOICE OF AN ANGEL

"Oh, God, please let this be a bad dream!"

Those were my only words as I paced the emergency room of St. Mary's Hospital. Our fifteen-month-old daughter, Tina, lay twitching on a table while the doctors tried to calm her little body. This was not how Thanksgiving Eve was supposed to be.

Earlier that evening, I had noticed Tina stirring in her bed and tiptoed to the crib to soothe and cover her, but to my horror, I realized that she was thrashing, jerking over and over, and unresponsive. Grabbing her up, I ran downstairs and frantically dialed our pediatrician, who told us to wrap her up and come immediately to the hospital.

The doctor met us at the doors of the emergency room, took our little one into her arms, and dashed away. Over her shoulder, she instructed us to "Just wait here—she's in good hands." According to the emergency room clock, it was 11:00 P.M.

MIRACLES OF DIVINE HEALING

My husband and I paced and prayed and watched the clock. How did we go from laughter over dinner to the emergency room with our daughter's life hanging in the balance? I remember saying, "I am going to wake up and I will be in my kitchen and Tina will be sleeping in her crib. This is just a bad dream."

It soon became clear, however, that this was no dream. I prayed, cried, and bargained with God, telling him how much I would change if he'd just spare Tina and, even though he'd get "the short end of the stick," would he please take me instead?

Shortly after 1:30 A.M., the doctor came out and spoke in soft, carefully chosen words. "It's taken us this long just to stabilize your daughter, and we still have no idea what has happened. It could be any number of things—a brain tumor, epilepsy, spinal meningitis, a stroke."

The doctor's words seemed to be coming at me in slow motion. "The thing is," she continued, "with that amount of pressure on the brain for that length of time, there is no way your child can be normal.

MIRACLES OF DIVINE HEALING

She could be blind, deaf, or disabled—any possibility and any combination. She's already paralyzed on the left side of her body. You need to be prepared for the worst. I'm sorry. We've done all we can do. It looks like you need a miracle."

My darling chatterbox toddler who brightened every room she entered—blind, deaf, disabled? My heart was broken and my body was numb.

They kept her in the hospital for two more weeks as they performed test after test—spinal taps, blood work, CAT scans. With no conclusion, very little hope, and a long list of medications, they sent us home to wait … wait for what? Something "significant"? Or just to see what fate God would bestow on this child?

We didn't have to wait long. Clearly, he chose healing. Every day Tina grew more responsive and her body less rigid. The spark in her eyes returned and so did her words (many and often). At her six-week checkup, she was talking up a storm, running around the doctor's office, and refusing to sit still. The doctor just shook her head and said, "Medically speaking,

MIRACLES OF DIVINE HEALING

there is no reason this child should be normal. It looks as though you've gotten your miracle."

A miracle indeed. Tina will celebrate her fortieth birthday soon. God had plans for her—plans to bless the multitudes with the singing voice of an angel (totally unbiased, you understand). For years, one dear friend has summed it up quite well. "Whenever Tina sings, I always have to smile with gratitude and relief as I remember the miracle that took place in Tina's life.[4]

MIRACLES OF DIVINE HEALING

I am the LORD, *who heals you.*

EXODUS 15:26

MIRACLES OF
DIVINE HEALING

He was pierced for our transgressions,
he was crushed for our iniquities;
the punishment that brought us
peace was upon him,
and by his wounds we are healed.

ISAIAH 53:5

MIRACLES OF DIVINE HEALING

─────── ⟨⟨∞⟩⟩ ───────

A RISK OF FAITH

After Jesus crossed over by boat, a large crowd met him at the seaside. One of the meeting-place leaders named Jairus came. When he saw Jesus, he fell to his knees, beside himself as he begged, "My dear daughter is at death's door. Come and lay hands on her so she will get well and live." Jesus went with him, the whole crowd tagging along, pushing and jostling him.

A woman who had suffered a condition of hemorrhaging for twelve years—a long succession of physicians had treated her, and treated her badly, taking all her money and leaving her worse off than before—had heard about Jesus. She slipped in from behind and touched his robe. She was thinking to herself, "If I can put a finger on his robe, I can get well." The moment she did it, the flow of blood dried up. She could feel the change and knew her plague was over and done with.

MIRACLES OF DIVINE HEALING

At the same moment, Jesus felt energy discharging from him. He turned around to the crowd and asked, "Who touched my robe?"

His disciples said, "What are you talking about? With this crowd pushing and jostling you, you're asking, 'Who touched me?' Dozens have touched you!"

But he went on asking, looking around to see who had done it. The woman, knowing what had happened, knowing she was the one, stepped up in fear and trembling, knelt before him, and gave him the whole story.

Jesus said to her, "Daughter, you took a risk of faith, and now you're healed and whole. Live well, live blessed! Be healed of your plague."

When he was still talking, some people came from the leader's house and told him, "Your daughter is dead. Why bother the Teacher any more?"

Jesus overheard what they were talking about and said to the leader, "Don't listen to them; just trust me."

MIRACLES OF
DIVINE HEALING

He permitted no one to go in with him except Peter, James, and John. They entered the leader's house and pushed their way through the gossips looking for a story and neighbors bringing in casseroles. Jesus was abrupt: "Why all this busybody grief and gossip? This child isn't dead; she's sleeping." Provoked to sarcasm, they told him he didn't know what he was talking about.

But when he had sent them all out, he took the child's father and mother, along with his companions, and entered the child's room. He clasped the girl's hand and said, "*Talitha koum,*" which means, "Little girl, get up." At that, she was up and walking around! This girl was twelve years of age. They, of course, were all beside themselves with joy. He gave them strict orders that no one was to know what had taken place in that room. Then he said, "Give her something to eat."[5]

The miracles of Jesus were the
ordinary works of his Father,
wrought small and swift that
we might take them in.

GEORGE MACDONALD

MIRACLES OF
DIVINE GUIDANCE

This God is our God for ever and ever;
he will be our guide even to the end.

PSALM 48:14

Jesus said, "My sheep listen to
my voice; I know them,
and they follow me."

J O H N   1 0 : 2 7

MIRACLES OF
DIVINE GUIDANCE

SOMEONE SPECIAL

Something exciting is going to happen today, I thought as I hurried into the airport. I was flying home, and a sense of expectancy convinced me that I was to meet someone special on the way home.

At boarding time, my anticipation grew. I eyed my fellow passengers as they lined up. Who could it be?

At the last moment before our flight took off, a flight attendant escorted a blond boy down the aisle and settled him into the aisle seat, one empty seat from me.

Was this the someone "special" I had been expecting? A boy? Just a boy? He looked about twelve years old.

He shot an unfriendly glance at me.

I turned to him. "Hi."

"Hi," he replied with a rapid glance in my direction.

"What's your name?" I asked, certain he resented my interest.

MIRACLES OF
DIVINE GUIDANCE

He barely turned toward me. "David."

I sat back again. That ended that. Clearly, I'd been wrong about having a special job on this trip home.

I tried to read my book, but couldn't concentrate.

The pilot announced, "Departure will be delayed for fifteen minutes due to a storm front over Chicago."

As we waited to leave, I decided to try again with my young seatmate who was reading the airline magazine.

"Is this your first plane trip?" I guessed, noting that he looked a little frightened.

He nodded, clutching the arm rests.

I began to talk to him to keep his mind off the plane. Finally David's fear eased, and he gazed out the window with me at the scenery.

Little by little, his story unfolded.

Though he had been separated from his mother since birth, his father and stepmother had decided to send him to live with her permanently—a frightening prospect for a twelve year old. In addition, there

MIRACLES OF
DIVINE GUIDANCE

would be a stepfather and two step siblings to adjust to. And I'd thought he was merely afraid of flying!

"I want to show you something," he said shyly. He unzipped his bag and pulled out his Bible and a book of children's Bible stories for me to see.

We discussed the pictures and the stories, delighting in each other's company. "My uncle gave me these books. He's a pastor," he told me. "My parents don't want to hear about God."

I fought tears, knowing that he and I would part in Chicago; a flight attendant would lead him to another plane.

"You know, David," I said, "when you love the Lord, he takes care of you, no matter where you are or what you're facing. Look at how he put us together for your first plane ride. It's a miracle that we'd sit in the same row."

He managed an uncertain smile.

"Do you suppose your uncle's been praying for you?"

MIRACLES OF
DIVINE GUIDANCE

"He said he would."

Our conversation drifted along pleasantly as we ate our lunches. David looked more at ease.

Shortly after the flight attendants cleared the trays, the pilot told everyone to be seated, and we descended into thick black storm clouds.

At first, streaks of lightning zigzagged through the dark sky; then we were in the midst of it. Lightning flashed wildly, illuminating our plane, flickering away, then bursting into eerie incandescence. We flew into the storm's fury, flying through its angry blasts and bucking like bronco riders.

Behind us, a man became ill. Across the aisle, a business man folded his hands in prayer.

I turned to David. What could I say at this moment when even adults' nerves failed? I thought of David's days ahead, too—an unknown mother and family, neighborhood, and school.

The answer came.

MIRACLES OF DIVINE GUIDANCE

"When you're scared," I told him, "say the name of Jesus over and over. He is always with you, and saying his name will remind you and give you peace."

David's eyes filled with hope. "I know it now," he said, "just like you being here, Jesus will take care of me."

Tears welled in my eyes and, ashamed, I recalled my first thought: A boy? Just a boy?

Our meeting was a miracle.

Smiling back at David, I was keenly aware that I'd met someone, who like all of us, is deeply loved by God.[6]

MIRACLES OF DIVINE HEALING

I am always with you;
you hold me by my right hand.
You guide me with your counsel.

PSALM 73:23–24

MIRACLES OF
DIVINE GUIDANCE

IN AND OUT OF SEASON

Several months before I joined a church group on a Reformation trip to Europe, a verse from the Bible haunted me: "Preach the word; be prepared in season and out of season."

Before long, that still small inner voice said, *Relearn your German.*

Relearn my German?

As a child, I'd learned the language from my German grandparents who had immigrated to Indiana. In college, I minored in German. Now, many years later, I was supposed to relearn it?

"Don't bother," friends told me. "Everyone in Europe speaks English."

In spite of their advice, I bought and listened to German-teaching CDs, relearning the alphabet, numbers, and commonly used words and phrases. But was this really useful work? To my surprise, my rusty German came in more handy than I could have imagined, and when we ended our ten-day trip in

MIRACLES OF DIVINE GUIDANCE

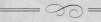

Munich, I realized the Lord had used me to tell five Germans, a Russian, and a German-American about him. Memories of castles, cathedrals, walled cities, and Reformation churches have since faded, but the joy of telling people about Jesus remains.

God's Word reminds us: "Preach the word; be prepared in season and out of season." And, yes, in *every* language *everywhere*. There are no coincidences, just miracles of understanding and salvation waiting when we listen and obey.[7]

MIRACLES OF DIVINE GUIDANCE

*All heaven is waiting to help
those who will discover the
will of God and do it.*

J. ROBERT ASHCROFT

MIRACLES OF DIVINE HEALING

God leads us step by step,
from event to event.
Only afterwards, as we look back over
the way we have come
and reconsider certain important
moments in our lives
in the light of all that has followed
them, or when we survey the whole
progress of our lives, do we experience
the feeling of having been led without
knowing it, the feeling that God has
mysteriously guided us.

PAUL TOURNIER

MIRACLES OF DIVINE GUIDANCE

AN UNUSUAL PROMPTING

As the office receptionist at Family Medical Clinic, I was finding it hard to maintain a cheerful demeanor with all the phone calls pouring in from needy patients. But my mood immediately improved as I saw Dr. Geller, one of my favorite docs.

"I thought you were off today, Dr. Geller."

"I was, but one of my favorite patients needs me."

"Who's that?" I asked.

He glanced down at the calendar and furrowed his white eyebrows. "Mrs. Blaine. As if cancer weren't enough, the poor woman needs an appendectomy."

"Mrs. Blaine? Oh, that poor woman. She has been through so much lately."

Feeling a burden, I offered up a word of prayer for her recovery from her appendectomy and continued my work. But as the day wore on, I found I couldn't shake the gentle, persistent nudging of the Holy Spirit. Finally, I realized the Holy Spirit was urging me to go and pray for her in person.

MIRACLES OF DIVINE GUIDANCE

When I arrived, Mrs. Blaine looked up and offered me one of her million-dollar smiles. "Well, look who's here," she waved a weak hand in my direction.

I smiled and sat nervously rubbing my fingers together. Finally, I confessed why I was there. "I just felt the Lord telling me to come and see you in person to pray for your healing."

A look of wonder came over Mrs. Blaine's face. "Well, what are you waiting for?" she asked.

I placed my hand on her arm and offered up a simple request for God's healing power to touch her body and make well all that was wrong with her.

A week went by and I had forgotten all about the incident with Mrs. Blaine, until Dr. Geller handed me her file.

"By the way," I asked, "how is Mrs. Blaine?"

"You didn't hear what happened to her?"

"No." My heart sank. *Could she have died?* I wondered.

"She's totally recovered!"

MIRACLES OF DIVINE GUIDANCE

"From her appendectomy?"

"From cancer! I did a blood screen and MRI on her a few days ago and the cancer is completely gone—truly a miracle."

I was speechless as the wonder of it filled my chest. Mrs. Blaine was healed!

I never told the doctor what I had done. Of course, my prayer was one of many that were offered up for her, but it was exciting to know that I had heard and obeyed God's guiding voice and had the honor of being part of a miracle.[8]

MIRACLES OF DIVINE GUIDANCE

God wants to bring us beyond the point where we need signs to discern his guiding hand. Satan cannot counterfeit the peace of God or the love of God dwelling in us. When Christ's abiding presence becomes our guide, then guidance becomes an almost unconscious response to the gentle moving of his Holy Spirit within us.

BOB MUMFORD

MIRACLES OF DIVINE GUIDANCE

A DIVINE ASSIGNMENT

An angel of the Lord said to Philip, "Go south to the road—the desert road—that goes down from Jerusalem to Gaza." So he started out, and on his way he met an Ethiopian eunuch, an important official in charge of all the treasury of Candace, queen of the Ethiopians. This man had gone to Jerusalem to worship, and on his way home was sitting in his chariot reading the Book of Isaiah the prophet. The Spirit told Philip, "Go to that chariot and stay near it."

Then Philip ran up to the chariot and heard the man reading Isaiah the prophet. "Do you understand what you are reading?" Philip asked.

"How can I," he said, "unless someone explains it to me?" So he invited Philip to come up and sit with him.

This is the passage of Scripture the eunuch was reading:

MIRACLES OF DIVINE GUIDANCE

"He was led like a sheep to the slaughter,
   and as a lamb before the shearer is silent,
      so he did not open his mouth.
In his humiliation he was deprived of justice.
Who can speak of his descendants?
For his life was taken from the earth."

The eunuch asked Philip, "Tell me, please, who is the prophet talking about, himself or someone else?" Then Philip began with that very passage of Scripture and told him the good news about Jesus.

As they traveled along the road, they came to some water and the eunuch said, "Look, here is water. What can stand in the way of my being baptized?" And he gave orders to stop the chariot. Then both Philip and the eunuch went down into the water and Philip baptized him. When they came up out of the water, the Spirit of the Lord suddenly took Philip away, and the eunuch did not see him again, but went on his way rejoicing.[9]

MIRACLES OF DIVINE GUIDANCE

*I am satisfied that when the
Almighty wants me to do or not to
do any particular thing, he finds a
way of letting me know.*

ABRAHAM LINCOLN

MIRACLES OF DIVINE GUIDANCE

*Jesus said, "When he,
the Spirit of truth, comes,
he will guide you into all truth."*

JOHN 16:13

MIRACLES OF
DIVINE GUIDANCE

*Whether you turn to the right or
to the left, your ears will hear a
voice behind you, saying,
"This is the way; walk in it."*

ISAIAH 30:21

This is a wise, sane Christian faith:
that a man commit himself,
his life, and his hopes to God; that
God undertakes the special protection
of that man; that therefore that man
ought not to be afraid of anything.

GEORGE MACDONALD

MIRACLES OF
DIVINE PROTECTION

—— ⚮ ——

May the LORD answer you
when you are in distress;
may the name of the
God of Jacob protect you.
May he send you help from the sanctuary
and grant you support from Zion.

PSALM 20:1–2

—— ⚮ ——

In the morning prayer is the key that opens to us the treasures of God's mercies and blessings; in the evening, it is the key that shuts us up under his protection and safeguard.

JACQUES ELLUL

MIRACLES OF
DIVINE PROTECTION

STAND STILL AND SEE!

Our dear cat, Calico, to go out at night for a few hours, but then she returns to the warm, secure, cat-dish-furnished house. But tonight she wasn't at the door when I opened it.

Outside, crickets and tree frogs chirped. Somewhere in the distance dogs barked. "Okay, girl," I called, "game's over. Come on out of your hiding place and get ready for bed."

Just then, two huge dogs came bounding down our street. Obviously they'd slipped off their leashes or broken out of their yards. Still calling Calico, I walked out to the end of our driveway.

Suddenly, out of nowhere, those two dogs hurled right up to our yard, stopping inches from me. One was a chow; the other, an ugly mixed breed, with powerful, rippling muscles.

I had expected them to wag their tails and whine to be petted. Instead, fangs were bared.

MIRACLES OF
DIVINE PROTECTION

I froze. The house was too far away for me to turn and run to it. And our street seemed absolutely deserted. I didn't know whether to scream or not. *God, please help me!* I prayed silently.

Right at that moment, I distinctly heard a voice say, *Stare at them! Don't lose control! Stand still and see the deliverance of the Lord!*

I was shaking so badly, I could hardly stand up. But I couldn't think of any alternatives. If I turned around, they'd be on my back in an instant. And if this voice was from God—who created those dogs in the first place—then I had better do what I was told.

So I did stand. And I stared as hard as I could.

Snarling and snapping, the two dogs stared back. Then they turned and headed down the street. I let my breath out. Safe!

But before I could move, they both whirled around and charged right back—leaping right up into the air in front of my face!

MIRACLES OF
DIVINE PROTECTION

Stand still! commanded the unseen voice. I was terrified but, through it all, I kept standing and staring.

Once again, those dogs stopped right where they were. And again they turned and started down the street.

I let out a big sigh of relief, just as I realized that the two howling monsters were headed toward me for the third time. This time, with a long, running leap, they hurled themselves at me with all their might. Incredibly, they did not touch me. Instead they fell backward as if they had been slapped away by an invisible hand.

Finally, snapping and growling with disgust, they left again. This time, they didn't return.

No wonder poor Calico had been hiding! In fact, it took me a full hour of coaxing before the frantic cat finally streaked in through our front door. It took that long for my own shakes to subside, as well.

MIRACLES OF
DIVINE PROTECTION

But my praise to my heavenly Father did not subside. He had not only told me what to do when I was too panic-stricken to think for myself, but he also gave me abundant power to do it. He instructed me and covered me with his guardian angel. An angel I couldn't see, but had overwhelming proof was there. "He will command his angels concerning you to guard you in all your ways" (Psalm 91:11).

I did stand still. And I did see the deliverance of the Lord. I witnessed a miracle.[10]

MIRACLES OF DIVINE PROTECTION

CHAIN ACCIDENT — MINUS ONE

A storm was closing in and it looked like a bad one, as midsummer afternoon thunderstorms in Michigan often are. I had borrowed a friend's car to visit a friend in need across state. The day had been tiring. Now I was on my way home.

Soon it began to rain in big splats—then half rain, half hail. As usual, the other drivers were driving too fast for the road conditions, especially since we had had a long dry spell and the consequent buildup of slick oil on the highway was becoming visible as it washed out of the hot pavement.

Suddenly the heavens cut loose. The rain came down in blinding sheets. I flipped the wipers onto their highest, most frantic setting, turned on my headlights, and peered through the windshield. It was like navigating a submarine through a carwash. The insides of the car windows began to steam up, but I couldn't do more than try to swipe at the glass right in front of my face to keep a small area clear.

MIRACLES OF DIVINE PROTECTION

As soon as the rain started, everyone had hit their brakes and red lights had blinked on ahead of me. But wait—now what was happening? As more red taillights appeared, I saw the hood of the car in front of me fly up into the rain, and then the trunk lid of the car ahead of that one. A car-top carrier ricocheted off to the side. I glimpsed headlights where I should have seen taillights.

Simultaneously and instantly, it was as if a pair of unseen hands grabbed my steering wheel and violently turned the car to the right—onto an exit ramp that "just happened" to be there. I glanced back at the expressway, where, in spite of the heavy rain, I could see—and hear—a chain-reaction collision in progress. My exit led me to one of those service roads that sometimes runs parallel to an expressway. I drove until I could pull off on the shoulder of the road, a little out of sight of the accident, and I stopped the car as calmly as if I had just pulled into my own driveway.

MIRACLES OF DIVINE PROTECTION

What had just happened? Evidently, God had sent one of his angels to steer me out of harm's way a split-second before impact. Certainly it would not have been my first instinct to steer myself off the road so abruptly. And I definitely could not have seen the exit right there.

The radio was still on, and it wasn't long before I heard the news about the accident. "On I–94 the storm has caused a massive pile-up. Reports from the scene say that from twenty to thirty cars are involved, with the possibility of more accidents as unaware drivers approach the scene at normal highway speeds."

Here I was, safe and sound, thanks be to God, without even a dent or a scratch on my borrowed car. I knew I had just experienced a miracle.[11]

MIRACLES OF
DIVINE PROTECTION

*The servants of Christ are protected
by invisible, rather than visible,
beings. But if these guard you,
they do so because they have been
summoned by your prayers.*

SAINT AMBROSE

MIRACLES OF DIVINE PROTECTION

GOD'S PEOPLE PROTECTED FROM MIGHTY ARMIES

The Moabites and Ammonites with some of the Meunites came to make war on Jehoshaphat. Alarmed, Jehoshaphat and the people of Judah came together to seek help from the LORD.

Then Jehoshaphat stood up and said: "O LORD, God of our fathers, are you not the God who is in heaven? You rule over all the kingdoms of the nations. Power and might are in your hand, and no one can withstand you. Did you not drive out the inhabitants of this land before your people Israel and give it forever to the descendants of Abraham your friend? They have lived in it and have built in it a sanctuary for your Name, saying, 'If calamity comes upon us, whether the sword of judgment, or plague or famine, we will stand in your presence before this temple that bears your Name and will cry out to you in our distress, and you will hear us and save us.'

MIRACLES OF DIVINE PROTECTION

"But now here are men from Ammon, Moab and Mount Seir, whose territory you would not allow Israel to invade when they came from Egypt; so they turned away from them and did not destroy them. See how they are repaying us by coming to drive us out of the possession you gave us. O our God, will you not judge them? For we have no power to face this vast army that is attacking us. We do not know what to do, but our eyes are upon you."

Then the Spirit of the LORD came upon Jahaziel. He said: "Listen, King Jehoshaphat and all who live in Judah and Jerusalem! This is what the LORD says to you: 'Do not be afraid or discouraged because of this vast army. For the battle is not yours, but God's. Tomorrow march down against them. You will not have to fight this battle. Take up your positions; stand firm and see the deliverance the LORD will give you. Do not be afraid; do not be discouraged. Go out to face them tomorrow, and the LORD will be with you.'"

MIRACLES OF DIVINE PROTECTION

Jehoshaphat bowed with his face to the ground, and all the people of Judah and Jerusalem fell down in worship before the LORD. Then some Levites stood up and praised the LORD with very loud voice.

Early in the morning they left for the Desert of Tekoa. As they set out, Jehoshaphat stood and said, "Listen to me, Judah and people of Jerusalem! Have faith in the LORD your God and you will be upheld; have faith in his prophets and you will be successful." After consulting the people, Jehoshaphat appointed men to sing to the LORD and to praise him for the splendor of his holiness as they went out at the head of the army, saying:

"Give thanks to the Lord,
    for his love endures forever."

As they began to sing and praise, the LORD set ambushes against the men of Ammon and Moab and Mount Seir who were invading Judah, and they were defeated. The men of Ammon and Moab rose up against the men from Mount Seir to destroy and

MIRACLES OF
DIVINE PROTECTION

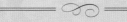

annihilate them. After they finished slaughtering the men from Seir, they helped to destroy one another.

When the men of Judah came to the place that overlooks the desert and looked toward the vast army, they saw only dead bodies lying on the ground; no one had escaped.[12]

MIRACLES OF DIVINE PROTECTION

GOD'S STORM SHELTER

On April 4, 1974, a series of violent tornadoes ripped through Alabama, leaving behind an unbelievable swath of destruction.

I was seventeen at the time, a junior in high school. My family and I lived in a small frame house situated in the middle of sprawling farmland, with cattle and horses grazing in the surrounding pastures. Normally I felt safe, but there was something eerily different about that April night.

There were a few storm warnings on television, but nothing issued for our area. My parents went to bed early, as did my five-year-old sister. My teenaged brother and I stayed up a little while longer, then said good night and headed to our rooms.

Unlike many southern homes, we had no storm cellar, and as I got ready for bed, I wondered just how secure we were. All I could do was pray that God would be with us and shelter us should the storms decide to blow our way.

MIRACLES OF DIVINE PROTECTION

I had been in bed for about ten minutes when I heard a distant rumbling and sat up to listen. Suddenly the ominous noise turned into a deafening roar. Without warning, a tornado had churned up in the skies a mile or so away and now bore down on us.

By the time I realized what was happening, our house began to rattle violently and shivered as if gripped in the jaws of some monstrous creature.

As the house trembled, the pressure in my room became almost unbearable. Terrified that the windows of my room would shatter, I threw my blankets over my head and huddled under them, crying desperately to God to protect us.

Unseen objects hammered the outer walls of the house unmercifully, and the roaring was relentless. My heart pounded and each breath became a struggle. I stared at the walls, expecting them to peel away before my eyes.

MIRACLES OF
DIVINE PROTECTION

Then, the sound began to fade. In a few moments, it had gone and the house stopped its terrible shivering. I jumped out of bed and rushed to meet my family in the living room. Everyone was shaken, but okay.

Early the next morning we filed outside to have a look at the house and yard. The screen door on the front had been slammed back so violently that the door handle was driven into the side of the house. There were a couple of cracked windows and a porch support was missing, as were some shingles from the roof. My sister's swing set teetered precariously on end, and my mom's Volkswagen bug sat a few feet from where she had left it parked.

We crossed the yard and turned to check out the back porch. It had sustained heavy damage and the furniture that had previously been arranged there now lay in pieces on the ground. Then I glanced toward the woods behind the house. What I saw took my breath away.

MIRACLES OF DIVINE PROTECTION

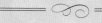

Coming from the woods was a line of enormous felled trees. They had been uprooted and were lying on their sides, their tangled root balls wrapped in huge chunks of damp, red earth. The trees made a straight line for the house—angled directly for the corner where my bedroom was. Miraculously, about fifty yards from the house, the row of fallen trees abruptly changed direction and headed to the right. More uprooted trees lay in a line leading away from the house.

My knees were shaking and my stomach twisted in knots, but my heart sang. Not only had God protected me and my family, but he left the evidence for all to see. Storm shelters saved thousands of lives that horrific night, but we didn't have one. What we did have was the most secure Shelter available; the strong hands of God that delivered us from the storm.[13]

MIRACLES OF DIVINE PROTECTION

God moves in a mysterious way his
wonders to perform;
He plants his footsteps in the sea,
and rides upon the storm.

WILLIAM COWPER

*God wishes each of us to work as
hard as we can, holding nothing back
but giving ourselves to the utmost,
and when we can do no more,
then is the moment when the hand
of Divine Providence is stretched
out to us and takes over.*

DON ORIONE

Miracles of Divine Provision

———— ✦ ————

Let us then fearlessly and confidently
and boldly draw near to the throne
of grace … that we may … find grace
to help in good time for every need
[appropriate help and well-timed
help, coming just when we need it].

Hebrews 4:16 AMP

———— ✦ ————

You will never need more than
God can supply.

J. I. PACKER

MIRACLES OF DIVINE PROVISION

THE FEEDING OF THE SOME-THOUSAND

Back when I was a new Christian and so were most of my friends, we expected God to intervene in our lives on a regular basis. And he did.

For instance, there was the time that we volunteered to help serve the first meal, which happened to be a lunch, at a large conference sponsored by a Christian group to which we belonged. There was only one problem: the lunch was going to be served as the conference registration process was underway in another part of the building, and nobody could accurately predict how many conferees would bring their meal tickets to the dining room.

"No problem. God will take care of it," we said blithely.

The caterer, Mr. Romanoff, wasn't so sure about that. He was the one who had to assemble the right amounts of each kind of food. And, wouldn't you

MIRACLES OF DIVINE PROVISION

know, he planned to serve submarine sandwiches for that first lunch. No way could he fiddle with portion size if the line of hungry customers happened to grow longer. He had brought a definite number of sandwiches, pre-made in his kitchen across town, to match a number that some conference-planner had pulled out of thin air.

In fact, Mr. Romanoff was hopping mad about this situation, as angry as an Italian caterer can be. His face was red, and he was literally stomping his feet as he chewed out his volunteer waitstaff (as if it was our fault). "You *people!*[sputter, sputter] I have a *reputation!*" But what could he do? It was too late to make more sandwiches; the queue of people was already forming at the door. And there was no Subway—or even a grocery store—within miles.

We meekly performed our assigned tasks. One volunteer collected the meal tickets and tallied them with a hand-held counter. The rest of us filled Styrofoam plates with the food: potato chips, raw

MIRACLES OF
DIVINE PROVISION

veggie sticks, cookies, and a whole, large submarine sandwich, bulging with meat, cheese, and toppings, on each person's plate. Our own stomachs were growling. We had been helping to set up the dining area all morning, and we had been told to expect a free lunch. Now it seemed obvious that, for us at the least, there would be no lunch after all.

The wrapped sandwiches were stowed in large blue plastic bakery trays that were piled on top of each other under the serving tables and hidden from view by floor-length white tablecloths. Whenever we finished distributing a tray full of sandwiches, we would add the empty tray to a pile behind the tables, reach under a table, and pull out a fresh tray.

The atmosphere behind the tables grew tenser as the line of customers grew longer. Apparently, the registration process upstairs was turning out to be way too efficient. Mr. Romanoff was prowling behind us like a police dog, glowering and muttering to himself, counting trays, returning to the ticket-

MIRACLES OF DIVINE PROVISION

taker to get the latest tally. We pasted smiles on our faces as we kept pulling out trays and serving … and serving … and serving.

Finally, the last person sat down with a full plate. It was time for the first conference session to begin. The doors to the dining room were closed. Maybe now we could nibble a few carrot sticks and go home?

We peeked under one of the serving tables. There, looking as fresh as the first batch, was another complete tray of submarine sandwiches. Trying not to even *look* like we were thinking, *We told you God would take care of it*, we filled our own plates and took them to a table in the far corner, while the disbelieving caterer inspected his towering pile of empty bakery trays.

Our God had multiplied the submarine sandwiches, which had become our modern-day equivalent of the loaves and the fishes. He had even, apparently, multiplied the plastic bakery trays! And he overshot in his abundant provision, because we had part of a tray of sandwiches left over.

MIRACLES OF DIVINE PROVISION

"They all ate and were satisfied, and the disciples picked up twelve basketfuls of broken pieces that were left over" (Matthew 14:20).

No question about it, Mr. Romanoff.[14]

MIRACLES OF DIVINE PROVISION

The LORD will guide you always;
he will satisfy your needs in a
sun-scorched land
and will strengthen your frame.
You will be like a well-watered garden,
like a spring whose waters never fail.

ISAIAH 58:11

MIRACLES OF DIVINE PROVISION

A WAY IN THE WILDERNESS

Like a hopeful pioneer, I loaded my three children in a station wagon and headed toward the sunset during the summer of 1991—looking to begin a new life. My family had passed through many difficult years at the hands of my former husband. In an effort to maintain control over us, he had made a habit of telling us that a woman alone with children was begging to be attacked by mass murderers and violent perverts. It was a difficult mindset to overcome, but I had been praying that God would help us conquer our fears. This trip seemed to be the answer.

The weather had been perfect and the car had been performing well—until we began to descend the mountains just north of San Francisco. The winding two-lane road that led toward the foothills was nearly deserted with no ditches.

Suddenly, steam began rolling off the car hood, and the temperature gauge registered in the red. I

MIRACLES OF
DIVINE PROVISION

knew immediately that we would have to stop some-where along the road—a terrifying thought.

Traveling a scant half a mile further, we encoun-tered a very large graveled roadside rest area. There was no telephone, and we were surrounded on all sides by heavily wooded mountains.

What are we going to do, I wondered as all the old fears came flooding back. *There is no one here to help us*.

It couldn't have been more than a few minutes before a van pulled over and stopped. A large burly man got out and leaned casually against the driver's side of his van.

"Looks like you got a problem, ma'am," he said in a matter-of-fact tone.

From my position about ten feet away, I looked him over carefully, memorizing his appearance. He seemed to be a workingman, and I judged that he stood about six feet tall. His fuzzy, reddish-brown hair was clean but unkempt. His shirtsleeves were rolled up, and he was wearing blue jeans.

MIRACLES OF
DIVINE PROVISION

"May I take a look?" he asked.

Waving the kids out of the car and back to the edge of the tree line, I quietly instructed them to be prepared to run into the woods and hide if anything weird happened.

The man raised the hood and removed the radiator cap. "You've got a leak in the radiator hose," he said. "You're out of water. I just returned from a job and I have something that might help you."

He returned to his van and pulled out a five-gallon bucket of water with no lid.

I almost laughed out loud, wondering what kind of person carries around an open five-gallon bucket of water in his truck.

The man poured the water into the radiator and replaced the lid.

"How far will it get me?" I asked.

"As far as you need to go," he answered. "Down the road, you'll come to a small town. At the intersection, turn right. Go to the second filling station—not the first. I know the owner there and he'll help you."

MIRACLES OF DIVINE PROVISION

With that small bit of advice, the man got into his van and pulled out onto the road.

I watched in astonishment and then signaled for the children to return to the car. "Get in quickly, kids!"

The van was just two cars ahead of us as we went around a curve. But as the highway opened up into a long stretch of open highway, we realized that the van and its driver had vanished. We looked for turnoffs but saw none. Nor did we pass any side roads.

Coming into a small town, we found the service station just as the man described. As the mechanic repaired the hose, I told him, "I really appreciate your friend helping me. It's so refreshing to find honest, considerate people." Then I described our rescuer.

"I don't know who that would be," the mechanic answered matter-of-factly.

"Maybe the owner of the station does. He said he knew the owner," I told him.

MIRACLES OF DIVINE PROVISION

"I'm the owner," he assured her, "and I don't know anyone who looks like that."

As I paid for the repairs, I said to the owner, "I want to thank you. The Lord's been good to us. You're an answer to prayer."

"Yes," said the mechanic, "he is good. He's my Lord and Savior, too."

Getting back on the road, the kids and I talked excitedly about the miracle we had just witnessed. God had been looking after us, and we knew he would continue to provide for us in the uncertain times to come."[15]

MIRACLES OF DIVINE PROVISION

My God will meet all your
needs according to his glorious
riches in Christ Jesus.

PHILIPPIANS 4:19

MIRACLES OF DIVINE PROVISION

THE TEACUPS ON A THOUSAND SHELVES

New to town and in a foolish move to get acquainted and be hospitable, I agreed to hostess a tea in my home. This, I thought, would be a piece of cake—served with tea or coffee.

In my imagination, I set the table with nice paper plates and coordinated napkins. Too late I realized that the coming guests were accustomed to having their crumpets served on genuine china.

I did own a small tea service, a common pattern from the 1940s called "Moss Rose." I frequently saw pieces for sale and felt it would be a small matter to buy up enough to competently serve the ladies.

So wrong! I searched at antique malls, auctions, garage sales, and flea markets in vain.

One sunny Saturday morning as I ran errands all over the countryside, I noticed the ditches were full of rummage sale signs. Antique auction signs too.

MIRACLES OF
DIVINE PROVISION

"Lord," I prayed aloud in my car, "you know where there is enough Moss Rose dishes to serve this tea. You have much bigger matters to tend to, I'm sure. But I believe that you do care about the little things in our lives. So I'm asking for your help." And then with an embarrassed chuckle, I asked God to place a golden arrow over the very place where I could find the treasures I was seeking.

In the next little burg, I could scarcely believe my eyes. There was a golden arrow! It was cardboard, but it was gold. Printed on it was "Garage Sale."

Following along, I soon came to a second golden arrow signaling toward a jumbled yard with rickety sawhorses supporting plywood sheets.

A voice inside me urged: *Ask! I said, ask!*

Reluctantly, I approached the lady of the house. As I described the china pattern I was looking for, the woman gave me a strange look.

"So you're the one. I have a tea set like that," she told me, "but I didn't put it out because I was waiting

MIRACLES OF DIVINE PROVISION

for the right person." She produced a few pieces from a hidden box. They were the Moss Rose pattern.

Marveling at God's sense of humor, I took them home. I was still one cup short, but did it matter? Perhaps God knew someone was not coming.

Later, as a friend and I ate lunch, I told her how God provided the tea set. We rejoiced in God's goodness. As we walked out of the restaurant door, we stopped short. On the hood of my car, something winked in the sunlight. A Moss Rose teacup!

I grilled numerous people I thought might be culpable and everyone denies any knowledge of the cup and how it came to be on the hood.

God does indeed own the teacups on a thousand shelves, and he sometimes uses them to serve up a miracle for even a silly woman like me!"[16]

MIRACLES OF DIVINE PROVISION

*You can be sure that God will take
care of everything you need,
his generosity exceeding even yours
in the glory that pours from Jesus.*

PHILIPPIANS 4:19 MSG

MIRACLES OF
DIVINE PROVISION

HIGH WATER IN HELL

August 1864—Andersonville, Georgia. On the flat, treeless field of red clay that made up the Confederate prison camp at Andersonville, ten thousand Union soldiers milled about. Many were naked and desperately ill. All, including the guards, were edging toward starvation.

In the heat of August, a torrent of prisoners were added to the prison population. One of those prisoners was eighteen-year-old Pvt. David Smith, First Battalion of the Pennsylvania Volunteers.

At the Battle of Piedmont, Virginia, David was wounded, shot ear to ear through the head. Bloody, covered with flies, unconscious, and mistaken for dead, he lay on the battlefield for three days and nights. Eventually, he was discovered and taken to Stauton, Virginia, where Confederate soldiers captured him and sent him to Andersonville Prison.

Although every human comfort was denied the prisoners, thirst was the worst torment. Not that the

MIRACLES OF DIVINE PROVISION

prison wasn't supplied with water. A thoroughly polluted creek meandered through the stockade giving the prisoners an awful choice: drink and take your chances with a multitude of plagues; abstain and die from thirst.

David Smith wrote: "Our supply of water was abominably filthy—beyond all description. I could attempt to describe it—but—I cannot without giving you needless offense and pain. During the month of August our suffering for water was very great."

Numerous contemporaries of Smith have verified what happened next.

David Smith wrote: " … now occurred one of the strangest happenings of my prison life. Famished for food, consumed with the indescribable fever of thirst, a few faithful Christians resolved to test the power of prayer.

"In their rags and wretchedness, and with tongues blistered by thirst, they prayed the God of heaven to send them water. And lo, while on their knees in

MIRACLES OF DIVINE PROVISION

the crawling sand, the clouds gathered and the rain gushed down in a refreshing shower. It was a terrific thunderstorm, in the nature of a waterspout.

"It was at this time Providence Spring first appeared, and it flows to this day, an everlasting testimonial to the power of prayer. It was the end of our suffering for water."

If you visit the site of Andersonville Prison, you will see Providence Spring.

David Smith survived both the head wound and Andersonville. He was exchanged November 20, 1864 at Savannah, Georgia. After his release from Andersonville, Smith served with the Union Army until his discharge on June 13, 1865.[17]

MIRACLES OF DIVINE PROVISION

The prayer of a righteous person is powerful and effective. Elijah was a human being, even as we are. He prayed earnestly that it would not rain, and it did not rain on the land for three and a half years. Again he prayed, and the heavens gave rain, and the earth produced its crops.

JAMES 5:16–18 TNIV

MIRACLES OF DIVINE PROVISION

ALWAYS PLENTY

The Lord said to Elijah, "Go to the east and hide by Cherith Brook.... Drink from the brook and eat what the ravens bring you, for I have commanded them to feed you."

So he did as the Lord had told him to and camped beside the brook. The ravens brought him bread and meat each morning and evening, and he drank from the brook. But after a while the brook dried up, for there was no rainfall anywhere in the land.

Then the Lord said to him, "Go and live in the village of Zarephath, near the city of Sidon. There is a widow there who will feed you."...

So he went to Zarephath. As he arrived at the gates of the city he saw a widow gathering sticks; and he asked her for a cup of water.

As she was going to get it, he called to her, "Bring me a bite of bread too."

MIRACLES OF DIVINE PROVISION

But she said, "I swear by the Lord your God that I haven't a single piece of bread in the house. And I have only a handful of flour left and a little cooking oil in the bottom of the jar. I was just gathering a few sticks to cook this last meal, and then my son and I must die of starvation."

But Elijah said to her, "Don't be afraid! Go ahead and cook that 'last meal,' but bake me a little loaf of bread first; and afterwards there will still be enough food for you and your son. For the Lord God of Israel says that there will always be plenty of flour and oil left in your containers until the time when the Lord sends rain and the crops grow again!"

So she did as Elijah said, and she and Elijah and her son continued to eat from her supply of flour and oil as long as it was needed. For no matter how much they used, there was always plenty left in the containers, just as the Lord had promised through Elijah![18]

MIRACLES OF DIVINE PROVISION

Jesus said, "Are not two sparrows sold
for a penny? Yet not one of them will
fall to the ground apart from the will
of your Father. And even the very
hairs of your head are all numbered.
So don't be afraid; you are worth
more than many sparrows.

MATTHEW 10:29–30

Come quickly to me, O God.
You are my help and my deliverer;
O LORD, do not delay.

PSALM 70:5

MIRACLES OF DIVINE DELIVERANCE

As for me, I know of nothing but miracles.

WALT WHITMAN

Jesus blew everything apart,
and when I saw where the pieces
landed, I knew I was free.

GEORGE BURMAN
FOSTER

MIRACLES OF DIVINE DELIVERANCE

FREE AT LAST

My miracle occurred in a parking lot on a January evening in 2001. God answered years of praying for my son, who had been enslaved by drug addiction and its roller coaster ride since he was an angry and unhappy teen.

He stopped me as I walked toward my car. "Mom, can I talk to you a minute?"

He was sober and well-groomed, with a peace in his face I hadn't seen in his thirty-eight years of life.

"I want to thank you for all the years you have prayed for me. I have truly surrendered my life to Jesus Christ."

Our son, now so obviously restored, had seldom called or visited his family. Even when we gathered for the holidays, he would show up high, intoxicated, or desperate for a "fix."

One day, after another chaotic holiday gathering in 1996, I poured out my grief to God in my journal. The entry is dated November 30.

MIRACLES OF
DIVINE DELIVERANCE

I finally saw him yesterday. It was awfully painful. He looks very sick. He was in an agitated state and making grandiose promises about his new job selling cemetery lots.

My peace and hope were knocked out of me with just one look at him. What he said didn't matter. I knew his words were lies and he couldn't keep his promises. The best I could do was sit and listen. He never looked at me directly, and I was glad. I couldn't have hidden my pain anyway.

Still, I'm grateful he's alive. I'm grateful he cares enough to come by, even for a little while, at the cost of facing his shame.

I don't know if anything I said or did got through. Probably not. But I don't know all things and I don't know how powerful my love and kindness are at this time. I saw my son through different eyes yesterday. I saw a very sick boy.

It was hard to hear him say he's been hungry and not say, 'Come here with me, son. I won't let you go hungry.' It was hard to hear he's losing weight and has

MIRACLES OF
DIVINE DELIVERANCE

a new 'friend' who moved in with him to 'help each other out.' Is this a true friend or is it someone who will exploit him? I don't know. I know it's useless to ask him any questions about it. Years ago, he said it while he was in a treatment center: 'It's the chemical talking, Mom.' Somewhere in that cocaine cloud is the son I know and love.

God, you will find him and save him. I don't know how or when, but I know you will.

A few weeks after the parking lot encounter, my son looked me in the eyes and proudly announced he had spoken about Jesus to a high school group and told his own story. At the time, I didn't know he arose at 5:00 A.M. every morning, drove twenty miles for an hour of intense Bible study with an older Christian man, and arrived at work by 8:00 A.M.

Each week my amazement increased at the changes in him; some from which I benefited with joy. If I needed my lawn mowed, my house painted, small repairs, or a house-sitter and cat-sitter when I went out of town, he was there.

MIRACLES OF DIVINE DELIVERANCE

Imagine the family's pride when we gathered for the celebration of his graduation with honors from the College of Biblical Studies.

Since the January evening in 2001 when he said, "I have truly surrendered my life to Jesus Christ," I've witnessed the powerful miracle of daily deliverance. My son is now the chemical-free man God intended him to be.[19]

MIRACLES OF
DIVINE DELIVERANCE

This is what the LORD says:
"Yes, captives will be taken
from warriors,
and plunder retrieved
from the fierce;
I will contend with those
who contend with you,
and your children I will save.

ISAIAH 49:25

MIRACLES OF DIVINE DELIVERANCE

Father, set me free in the glory of thy will, so that I will only as thou willest. Thy will be at once thy perfection and mine. Thou alone art deliverance—absolute safety from every cause and kind of trouble that ever existed, anywhere now exists, or ever can exist in thy universe.

GEORGE MACDONALD

MIRACLES OF DIVINE DELIVERANCE

DELIVERED OF A
TROUBLESOME SPIRIT

Once when we were going to the place of prayer, we were met by a slave girl who had a spirit by which she predicted the future. She earned a great deal of money for her owners by fortune-telling. This girl followed Paul and the rest of us, shouting, "These men are servants of the Most High God, who are telling you the way to be saved." She kept this up for many days.

Finally Paul became so troubled that he turned around and said to the spirit, "In the name of Jesus Christ I command you to come out of her!" At that moment the spirit left her.[20]

MIRACLES OF DIVINE DELIVERANCE

*God just doesn't throw a life pre-
server to a drowning person. He goes
to the bottom of the sea, and pulls
a corpse from the bottom of the sea,
takes him up on the bank, breathes
into him the breath of life and makes
him alive. That's what the Bible says
happens in your salvation.*

R. C. SPROUL

MIRACLES OF DIVINE DELIVERANCE

I DO BELIEVE!

On numerous occasions during the ten years my friend Eve Padilla had been a believer in Christ, she talked with her father about her relationship with God, but to no avail.

Then in April 1995, at age 63, Eve's father developed a severe case of diabetes and a sore on his left foot. By the time he sought medical care, toxins had spread throughout his body, leaving the doctors no choice but to amputate the foot.

As the only Christian in her family, Eve often prayed for her father. Then God answered her prayer in an unexpected way.

In the summer of 1995, Eve's father, Bill, was told that his right leg would have to be amputated, as well. Without the surgery, Bill would not survive—and yet the surgery itself might kill him. It was at this life-or-death moment that Eve summoned prayer warriors.

MIRACLES OF DIVINE DELIVERANCE

"There is a ladies' prayer chain in town," said Eve. "I explained the situation to the leader and asked them to pray for my dad. What I didn't know until later was that they agreed together in prayer that Dad wouldn't die unless he was assured of going to heaven." That prayer would become the pivotal point in Bill Anderson's eternal future.

As Bill's family waited outside the operating room, a nurse greeted them with very bad news.

"Your dad died on the operating table," she told them solemnly, "but we were able to revive him. You need to see him now because he's isn't going to be alive very much longer."

Although he was now missing both legs and attached to a labyrinth of tubes, to Eve, Bill Anderson still appeared to be the big, stocky man he always had been—until he opened his eyes and looked directly into Eve's.

A tube in his throat inhibited his speech, and he made motions that he wanted to write. In ragged but

MIRACLES OF DIVINE DELIVERANCE

readable script, he penned, "If I make it through this, there will be major changes in my life."

"Dad, did you die?" Eve asked him.

Although there was a burst of anguished tears, Bill's eyes remained open wide with fright. He nodded.

"Did you see heaven?"

Slowly, looking only at Eve, he shook his head.

Eve leaned down close to her father's ear as she tenderly held his hand. "We prayed, Dad. I don't believe this is your time to die. I hope you can believe it, too."

By the next morning, to everyone's surprise, Bill's condition had stabilized and they were able to remove the respirator. Although still in the intensive care unit, he was waiting anxiously for his family to arrive. He had something to say.

Weak, but sitting upright in bed, Bill told his children about his death only the day before. He described how he had floated above the doctors and

MIRACLES OF DIVINE DELIVERANCE

saw his own body, sans both legs, lying lifeless on the operating table.

As the realization dawned that he was dead, his soul moved into a long, dark tunnel. Quickly he realized he was not on his way to heaven.

"Now do you know what I've been telling you is true?" asked Eve. "Are you ready to accept Christ?"

While her family looked on, Eve prayed the simple sinner's prayer with Bill.

For the next years of his life, Bill told his story to many with whom he came into contact—a story of deliverance from doubt and the miracle of believing.[21]

MIRACLES OF DIVINE DELIVERANCE

*The final heartbeat for the Christian
is not the mysterious conclusion to a
meaningless existence.
It is, rather, the grand beginning to
a life that will never end.*

JAMES DOBSON

I write this to you whose experience
with God is as life-changing as ours,
all due to our God's straight dealing
and the intervention of our
God and Savior, Jesus Christ.

2 PETER 1:1 MSG

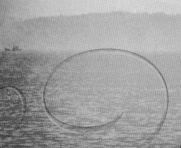

MIRACLES OF
DIVINE INTERVENTION

~§~

Long my imprisoned spirit lay
Fast bound in sin and nature's night.
Thine eye diffused a quickening
ray I woke,
the dungeon flamed with light.
My chains fell off, my heart was free.
I rose, went forth,
and followed Thee.

CHARLES WESLEY

~§~

The angels are the dispensers and administrators of the divine beneficence toward us; they regard our safety, undertake our defense, direct our ways, and exercise a constant solicitude that no evil befalls us.

JOHN CALVIN

MIRACLES OF
DIVINE INTERVENTION

STRANGER ON A FENCEPOST

Pulling his coat tight against the bitter wind, the old man stopped at the crest of Blue Bank Hill, near Flemingsburg, Kentucky. Above him, the winter sky pinked with the first blush of dawn. A blush reflected in the snow all around him—and in the treacherous ice beneath his feet.

Just in front of him, the road dropped off like a rollercoaster—a rollercoaster coated with deadly ice! Beside him, his weary mules chomped at their bits, their warm breath forming instant puffs in the freezing air. Behind him loomed the wagonload of railroad ties they had been pulling ever since four o'clock that morning along twisting, unpaved Eastern Kentucky mountain roads. Ties that he himself had logged and dressed from his own forest. For though already seventy-five, Reason ("Reece") Hinton was still as strong and ramrod-straight as a man half his age.

MIRACLES OF
DIVINE INTERVENTION

But strong enough to make it down that hill without losing his wagon, his load, his mules—or even his own life? If only he'd known about this ice back when he'd left home! Then he could have asked one of his sons or grandsons along.

Though he probably *wouldn't* have. For unfortunately, Reece Hinton was a stubborn man, to his usual regret. But, somehow, God always managed to come through to help him out of all his difficulties.

He needed every ounce of energy possible to keep his wagon from careening out of control on the way down. Not enough brake action invited a wild (and possibly deadly) plunge. Too much could lock the wheels, jerking them sideways—and pitching those heavy logs forward onto his helpless mules.

Still praying, he spoke encouragingly to the protesting animals, then clicked the reins. As they lunged, he jerked the wooden brake stick back and forth to maintain control.

MIRACLES OF
DIVINE INTERVENTION

Inch by inch they moved forward. Then suddenly the wagon began gaining momentum, while the mules fought in vain for footing on the slick ice.

Desperately now, Reece fought with the brake — his fingers almost frozen from the cold and effort. But between the ice and the down slope and the rapidly increasing speed, he was quickly losing the battle.

"Dear God!" he prayed out loud. "If you're going to help me, please do it *quickly*!"

In answer, "Hey, there, mister, could you-all use an extra hand?"

Jerking around, he saw a farmer sitting on a fencepost beside the road. Not even stopping to ask why anyone should be out there this bitterly cold morning, Reece yelled back, "Sure could, son."

Reece expected the man to help with the reins up front or pull back on the wagon from behind. Instead, the stranger just put his hand up on the wagon side and walked companionably alongside it in the snow.

MIRACLES OF DIVINE INTERVENTION

But something remarkable happened. Instantly the mules stopped sliding; the wagon stopped skidding. They could have been traveling on flat ground!

The two men continued talking about mules and lumber and things of the Lord all the way down the hill. At the bottom, the stranger said, "Well, guess I'd better go now."

The old man reached for his new friend's hand. But there was no one there. Now that all danger was over, the stranger had simply vanished into thin air.

As soon as he returned home to his farm in Muses Mills late that night, Reece told his daughter Alice and granddaughter, Ruby, about this wonderful stranger, insisting that God had miraculously saved his life by sending an angel to help him that bitter, icy morning.[22]

MIRACLES OF DIVINE INTERVENTION

If you pray truly, you will feel within yourself a great assurance: and the angels will be your companions.

EVAGRIUS OF PONTUS

MIRACLES OF DIVINE INTERVENTION

*A miracle is a work exceeding the
power of any created agent,
consequently being an effect of
the divine omnipotence.*

ROBERT SOUTH

MIRACLES OF
DIVINE INTERVENTION

══════ ∞ ══════

LISA'S ANGEL

We'd gone to bed, but I was still worried about my daughter. Only weeks after graduating from a university, she'd moved on her own to Washington, DC. I never turned on the news because I didn't like to hear about muggings, murder, and rape. Did Lisa understand what it meant to be young and single, boarding subways at night, and living alone?

Tonight I was worried, and I'd been talking to my husband about it until finally he'd gone to bed. He'd fallen asleep almost immediately, and now it was time for me to sleep, as well. But I couldn't. Instead, I prayed.

"Father, I'm worried about Lisa," I whispered. "She trusts you. *Please* take care of her."

Crushing and reshaping my pillow, I had just closed my eyes when I heard a whisper in my spirit. *Pray for an angel for Lisa*, it said—and I bolted upright as, on the heels of what I hadn't yet processed,

MIRACLES OF
DIVINE INTERVENTION

a second "thought" followed the first. *Pray she does not go through the tunnel.*

"Scotty!" I nearly shouted, shaking my husband's shoulder. "We need to pray for Lisa," I cried, as my husband bolted upright, too.

Scotty stared at me for several seconds before he took my hand. "She'll be okay, babe," he said, as we bowed our heads.

Though I couldn't stop shaking, together we recalled God's promises—told him we had read his Word, and we believed that Word when it said his angels encamp round about those who fear him. We also reminded ourselves that he takes care of his own.

Five minutes after midnight, the phone rang. Picking up the receiver, I heard my daughter's voice. "Mom!" she cried. "There was an *angel* on my train! There was no one else at my bus stop when I left work," she was saying. But when she'd transferred to the Metro? "He was on the train!" When she first

MIRACLES OF
DIVINE INTERVENTION

spotted him just sitting there, she'd felt frightened. She'd boarded at the end of the line. Where had this person come from?

"But then he looked at me, and he had the most beautiful eyes." I envisioned my daughter smiling. "I've never seen eyes like his before, Mom, and then he started to speak, but it didn't seem like he could hear." Just a man who was deaf, she'd thought at first. "But he wasn't just a man, Mom," Lisa said.

I wanted to speak, but I couldn't, and now Lisa was saying he'd told her that her life had been difficult. He was right, it had been. But it was going to become good, she wasn't to be afraid.

"And, Mom?" Lisa quickly continued, "I got off the train. You know where."

I certainly did, it gave me chills just thinking.

"And I started toward the tunnel." Lisa paused. "But, Mom, something kept saying, '*Don't go through the tunnel. Don't go through the tunnel.*'" *Don't go through the tunnel?* My mouth dry, I began to tell my

MIRACLES OF
DIVINE INTERVENTION

daughter about the prayers we'd just prayed. When we were both too tired to talk, I placed the receiver back down. *Pray for an angel and don't go through the tunnel?* Had God actually put an angel on my daughter's train?

Not until several days had passed did I receive what, for me, was my answer. It was then that I wholly understood that God had, in fact, performed a miracle of intervention on behalf of my child.

My husband had been in Washington for a meeting where he'd purchased a paper—and on a middle page, I read the report. A rapist who'd eluded the police for months had finally been arrested—just a stone's throw from the tunnel.[23]

MIRACLES OF DIVINE INTERVENTION

*Angels guard you when you walk
with Me. What better way could
you choose?*

FRANCES J. ROBERTS

MIRACLES OF DIVINE INTERVENTION

All is well, tho faith and form
Be sundered in the night of fear;
Well roars the storm
to those that hear
A deeper voice across the storm.

ALFRED, LORD
TENNYSON

MIRACLES OF DIVINE INTERVENTION

JESUS STILLS THE STORM

One day Jesus said to his disciples, "Let's go over to the other side of the lake." So they got into a boat and set out. As they sailed, he fell asleep. A squall came down on the lake, so that the boat was being swamped, and they were in great danger.

The disciples went and woke him, saying, "Master, Master, we're going to drown!"

He got up and rebuked the wind and the raging waters; the storm subsided, and all was calm.

"Where is your faith?" he asked his disciples.

In fear and amazement they asked one another, "Who is this? He commands even the winds and the water, and they obey him."[24]

*Do not conform any longer to the
pattern of this world, but be
transformed by the renewing of your
mind. Then you will be able to test
and approve what God's will is —
his good, pleasing and perfect will.*

ROMANS 12:2

MIRACLES OF DIVINE TRANSFORMATION

We, who with unveiled faces all reflect the Lord's glory, are being transformed into his likeness with ever-increasing glory, which comes from the Lord, who is the Spirit.

2 CORINTHIANS 3:18

*I never have any difficulty believing
in miracles, since I experienced the
miracle of a change in my own heart.*

SAINT AUGUSTINE
OF HIPPO

MIRACLES OF DIVINE TRANSFORMATION

A GRANDFATHER'S HEART

"I just want you to realize that if you and Alice adopt, it won't be the same. The child will not have your blood," George told Benny in Spanish.

The well-meaning words pierced like a knife as Benny listened to a man he had always respected—his father. But after seven years of fertility testing and surgeries, we longed for a child.

Just weeks earlier, we had met a young lady who was looking for a Christian couple to adopt her baby. Janie was five months along and wanted the mother-to-be to be present in the delivery room.

Excitedly, we accepted and waited for the baby's arrival. Now Benny and I attempted to prepare our families for the special event that would soon take place.

As time drew near, we kept our families up to date on all the exciting events. Finally, more than two weeks late, we received a call that Janie was in labor! Benny and I drove to the hospital. I stayed by her side

MIRACLES OF DIVINE TRANSFORMATION

as her labor progressed. At 5:56 the next morning, Veronica Jo was born—all 9 pounds and 12 ounces.

Immediately after the birth, a nurse bundled the baby up for her mother to hold. Janie, however, weary and exhausted, lifted her hand to point in my direction and said, "Let her hold the baby first!"

Weak and trembling from lack of sleep, I stretched out my arms. I gazed down into the baby's little face, praising God for the gift of life. After a few moments I passed her to Benny. We couldn't wait to take her home.

We visited Veronica each day in the hospital. On the third day of her life, we drove home with Veronica in her car seat. In the next few weeks, we fell in love with our precious baby girl.

At three months of age, we took Veronica on her first trip to meet her Texas family. When we arrived at Benny's parents' home, everyone was there.

Not long after our arrival, George took Veronica in his big, burly arms. Benny held his breath as he watched his father's eyes lock on her tiny face.

MIRACLES OF DIVINE TRANSFORMATION

He seemed to love her right away. After supper, Benny spotted George once again holding and cuddling Veronica. He made his way to his father's side, and soon the two men were playing with her and answering her coos.

Finally, George looked at Benny and said, "*No hay diferencia!*" That is to say, "There is no difference!" Understanding filled his eyes as he looked down at his new little granddaughter.

Three years later God blessed us with more children! Twins Mark and Rachel are also adopted; however, you would never know it by looking at our family reunions. There was always plenty of love to go around, especially from George.

Some might not call this a miracle—but we do. God transformed my father-in-law's mind and opened his heart to give and receive love in a new way. We will always be grateful.[25]

MIRACLES OF DIVINE TRANSFORMATION

*Faith means being grasped by a
power that is greater than we are,
a power that shakes us and turns
us, and transforms and heals us.
Surrender to this power is faith.*

PAUL JOHANNES
OSKAR TILLICH

MIRACLES OF DIVINE TRANSFORMATION

TOTALLY CHANGED

Paul,… eager to destroy every Christian, went to the High Priest in Jerusalem. He requested a letter addressed to synagogues in Damascus, requiring their cooperation in the persecution of any believers he found there.…

As he was nearing Damascus on this mission, suddenly a brilliant light from heaven spotted down upon him! He fell to the ground and heard a voice saying to him, "Paul! Paul! Why are you persecuting me? … I am Jesus, the one you are persecuting! Now get up and go into the city and await my further instructions."

The men with Paul stood speechless with surprise, for they heard the sound of someone's voice but saw no one! As Paul picked himself up off the ground, he found that he was blind. He had to be led into Damascus and was there three days, blind, going without food and water all that time.

MIRACLES OF DIVINE TRANSFORMATION

Now there was in Damascus a believer named Ananias. The Lord spoke to him in a vision, calling, "Ananias!"

"Yes, Lord!" he replied.

And the Lord said, "Go ... find the house of a man named Judas and ask there for Paul of Tarsus."

"But Lord," exclaimed Ananias, "I have heard about the terrible things this man has done to the believers in Jerusalem!"

But the Lord said, "Go and do what I say. For Paul is my chosen instrument to take my message to the nations."

So Ananias went over and found Paul and laid his hands on him and said, "Brother Paul, the Lord Jesus ... has sent me so that you may be filled with the Holy Spirit and get your sight back."

Instantly ... Paul could see and was immediately baptized.... He ... went at once to the synagogue to tell everyone there the Good News about Jesus—that he is indeed the Son of God![26]

MIRACLES OF DIVINE TRANSFORMATION

The wages of sin is death,
but the gift of God is eternal life
in Christ Jesus our Lord.

ROMANS 6:23

MIRACLES OF DIVINE TRANSFORMATION

When someone becomes a Christian,
he becomes a brand new person
inside. He is not the same anymore.
A new life has begun!

2 CORINTHIANS 5:17 TLB

MIRACLES OF DIVINE TRANSFORMATION

WHEN I WAS SEVENTEEN

With my books resting in my left arm, my right arm swung happily as I walked down the hall. I smiled at as many approaching students as I could, anyone who would meet my glance. I was after that award: the peace pipe, given to the girl designated "Friendliest Junior." I had forced myself to learn to meet people's eyes, to smile at them.

I slid into my seat in history. I flicked my long hair back over my shoulders and sat up attentively. I wanted to look the part of the good student, as well as get the grades. I raised my hand to answer his first question.

At the end of the school year, I nonchalantly tossed my report card down on the table at home. My parents would be pleased, but I wouldn't make a big deal out of it—no sense embarrassing my sisters, who would get good report cards, too, but probably not quite as good as mine. And I won the peace pipe. It sat on my dresser all the next year.

MIRACLES OF DIVINE TRANSFORMATION

During the summer, I went away to music camp. Nobody there knew about my grades or my peace pipe, but I played clarinet pretty well. I wouldn't tell them about my other achievements — unless they asked.

After rehearsal one evening, I walked back to the dorm with Joe, a trumpet player. My new friend asked, "Do you go to church?"

"Mm-hmm." All my life — week in, week out.

"So what does your church believe?"

"Umm …" For the first time in my life, this smart girl had no answer.

"Well, what do *you* believe?"

When I still said nothing, Joe began very gently to tell me what he believed.

"Everyone has sinned — everyone! We all need Jesus, because as hard as we might try, none of us is able to live a perfect life. Jesus Christ lived it for us."

My mind whirled. My stomach knotted as I thought of my good-girl image: I didn't smoke, I didn't drink,

MIRACLES OF DIVINE TRANSFORMATION

do drugs, or have sex. I had great grades, a good reputation, and a peace pipe for being friendly.

But I remembered my pride as I sauntered through
those high school halls. I stared at the ground as we
walked; I didn't want Joe to see the tears welling up.

"So would you like to?"

"Would I like to … what?"

"Ask Jesus to wash you clean on the inside and give
you new life?

I nodded numbly. Joe closed his eyes. Simply and
slowly, he led me in prayer. I traded in my puny goodness for Jesus' perfection, my pride for his humility,
my inner sinfulness for his inner cleansing.

Over the last thirty years, the Lord has met me
time after time. But what miracle could be greater
than the one that transformed my life the year I was
seventeen?[27]

*A miracle is a law-abiding event by
which God accomplishes his redemp-
tive purposes through the release of
energies which belong to a plane of
being higher than any with which we
are normally familiar.*

LESLIE WEATHERHEAD

Jesus said, "believe me when I say
that I am in the Father and the
Father is in me; or at least believe on
the evidence of the miracles themselves. I tell you the truth, anyone
who has faith in me will do what
I have been doing. He will do even
greater things than these,
because I am going to the Father.

JOHN 14:11–12

NOTES

1. *"What's for Dinner?"* by Rosi Braatz, Lakeville, Minnesota. Used by permission of the author.
2. *A Miracle for Melodie* by Golda Browne, Tulsa, Oklahoma. Used by permission of the author.
3. *Healing Prayer* by Deborah Webb, Bentonville, Arkansas. Used by permission of the author.
4. *The Voice of an Angel* by Rosi Braatz, Lakeville, Minnesota. Used by permission of the author.
5. *A Risk of Faith,* Mark 5:21–43 MSG.
6. *Someone Special* by Elaine L. Schulte, Tucson, Arizona. Used by permission of the author.
7. *In and Out of Season* by Elaine L. Schulte, Tucson, Arizona. Used by permission of the author.
8. *An Unusual Prompting* by Therese Stenzel, Tulsa, Oklahoma. Used by permission of the author.
9. *A Divine Assignment,* Acts 8:26–39 TNIV.
10. *Stand Still and See!* by Bonnie Compton Hanson, Santa Ana, California. Used by permission of the author.
11. *Chain Accident — Minus One* by Kathryn R. Deering, Ann Arbor, Michigan. Used by permission of the author.
12. *God's Pepole Protected from Mighty Armies,* 2 Chronicles 20:1, 3–12, 14–24
13. *God's Storm Shelter* by Anne Culbreath Watkins, Vermont, Alabama. Used by permission of the author.
14. *The Feeding of the Some-thousand* by Kathryn R. Deering, Ann Arbor, Michigan. Used by permission of the author.
15. *A Way in the Wilderness* by Rebekah Montgomery, Kewanee, Illinois. Used by permission of the author.
16. *The Teacups on a Thousand Shelves* by Rebekah

Montgomery, Kewanee, Illinois. Used by permission of the author.

17. *High Water in Hell* by Rebekah Montgomery, Kewanee, Illinois. Used by permission of the author. David Smith's account of Andersonville's Providence Spring was written out longhand in manuscript form and is in his family's possession.

18. *Always Plenty* 1 Kings 17:2–16 TLB.

19. *Free at Last,* Dee Smith, Houston, Texas. Used by permission of the author.

20. *Delivered of a Troublesome Spirit*, Acts 16:16–18.

21. *I Do Believe!* by Rebekah Montgomery, Kewanee, Illinois. Used by permission of the author.

22. *Stranger on a Fencepost* by Bonnie Compton Hanson, Santa Ana, California. Used by permission of the author. *While doing some research on my family's background, I learned of this incident, which happened about 1929, from a aunt of mine, Ruby Hinton Compton, now of Sun City Center, Florida. The Reece Hinton of the story was Ruby's and my father's maternal grandfather, my own great-grandfather. He lived with Ruby and her mother after his wife died.*

23. *Lisa's Angel* by Nancy Hoag, Bozeman, Montana. Used by permission of the author.

24. *Jesus Stills the Storm*, Luke 8:22–25.

25. *A Grandfather's Heart* by Alice Benavides, Jenks, Oklahoma. Used by permission of the author.

26. *Totally Changed*, Acts 9:1–11, 13, 15, 17–20 TLB.

27. *When I Was Seventeen* by Jacqueline Kuehn, Lucernemines, Pennsylvania. Used by permission of the author.

At Inspirio, we would love to hear your stories and your feedback. Please send your comments to us by way of email at

icares@zondervan.com

or to the address below:

Attn: Inspirio Cares
5300 Patterson Avenue SE
Grand Rapids, MI 49530

If you would like further information about Inspirio and the products we create, please visit us at:
www.inspiriogifts.com

Thank you and God bless!